Why is it dark at night?

DK Direct Limited
Managing Art Editor Eljay Crompton
Senior Editor Rosemary McCormick
Writer Alexandra Parsons
Illustrators The Alvin White Studios and Richard Manning
Designers Wayne Blades, Veneta Bullen, Richard Clemson,
Sarah Goodwin, Diane Klein, Sonia Whillock

Printed in the United States of America
ISBN:1-56326-221-5

Contents

MICKEY

Why is it dark at night?

Because at night the part of the world where we live has turned away from the sun. Although we cannot feel it, our planet is spinning in space. It takes a day and a night to turn full circle. So the side of the earth that is facing the sun is having daylight, and on the other side it's – goodnight!

Night and day facts

- On June 21, the northern half of the earth has its longest day and its shortest night.
- The shortest day and the longest night is on December 21.

Sun gods
Many peoples once worshiped sun gods. This is an ancient South American ceremonial mask of a sun god.

Why is it cold in winter?

It's because the earth isn't only spinning to give us night and day, it is also traveling around the sun in a big circle. It takes a whole year to go all the way round. For about half the year the bottom part of the earth is leaning away from the sun, so it's colder there. The top half is closer to the sun and warmer.

What time is it?
How does a witch
tell the time?
With a witch watch!

Changing seasons

The closer you live to the middle of the earth, the less the weather changes. But further away, the weather is more changeable and there are different seasons. Do you know the names of the seasons and what the weather is like in each?

Tilt!
Did you know that the earth is slightly tilted? And it spins around an imaginary line drawn through the north and south poles. This line is called an axis.

When it's lunchtime in California, what time is it in New York?

Almost dinnertime! As the earth spins around, light from the sun spreads slowly across the earth, reaching one country after another. So the day starts at different times. The earth is divided into 24 time zones, each one an hour later than its neighbor to the west. America is so big, it covers six time zones.

Traveling through time

- If a very fast aircraft could travel at the same speed as the turning of the earth, it would stay in sunlight all day and night. Time would seem to stand still on board because the day would never end.
- Time zones, as they exist today, were needed because of the development of railways carrying people very far, very fast.

From sea to shining sea
Which time zone do you live in?

How did people long ago tell the time?

Well, they didn't have clocks or watches, so they watched the sun. They saw that when the sun moved across the sky, shadows moved around on the ground, too. They discovered that if they measured the movement of the shadows, they could measure time. So they made shadow "clocks" called sundials.

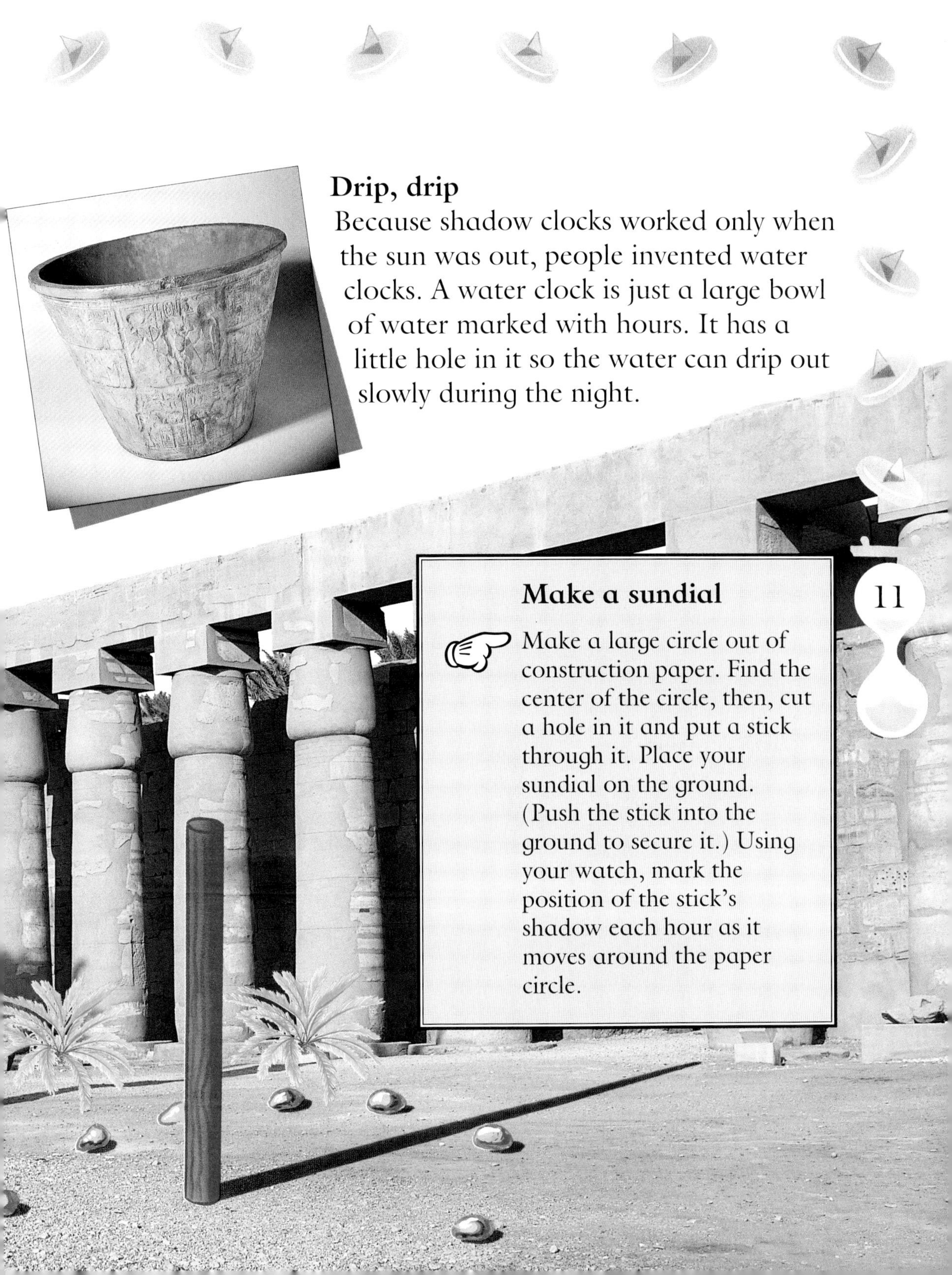

Drip, drip

Because shadow clocks worked only when the sun was out, people invented water clocks. A water clock is just a large bowl of water marked with hours. It has a little hole in it so the water can drip out slowly during the night.

Make a sundial

Make a large circle out of construction paper. Find the center of the circle, then, cut a hole in it and put a stick through it. Place your sundial on the ground. (Push the stick into the ground to secure it.) Using your watch, mark the position of the stick's shadow each hour as it moves around the paper circle.

When were clocks invented?

Nearly 700 years ago! The very first mechanical clocks didn't have hands or a dial. They were powered by weights and they told the time by ringing a bell. Later, they were used as alarm clocks to get monks out of bed, or in from the fields, to pray.

Special clocks
This is an old grandfather clock. Grandfather clocks have a pendulum inside which swings back and forth. Many make a lovely chiming sound on the hour.

Time tickler
What did the clockmaker say to the broken clock?
We have ways of making you tock!

Clocks and more clocks

- Long ago, only very rich and important people had clocks.
- Nearly 500 years ago, some clocks were made that were small enough for a person to carry around. In a way, these were the first watches.
- The largest clock in the world is in France. It's larger than a giraffe!

Why do we have months?

Months are how we measure the movements of the earth and the moon. A month is about as long as it takes for the moon to circle the earth. In fact the word month is based on the word moon. Do you know how many months there are in a year?

Name that month
Did you know that the month of July is named after the Roman emperor Julius Caesar?

Months and months
Which month of the year has 28 days?
All of them!

Can you remember this?

Here's a rhyme to help you remember how many days there are in each month: "Thirty days has September, April, June, and November. All the rest have 31, except for February which has 28 days, dear, and 29 in each leap year."

Why does the moon change shape?

It doesn't! The moon is as round as the earth, but we only see the parts of it that are lit up by the sun. The shape of the moon that we see is the shape of the sun's light hitting a certain part of the moon. During a month you will see different moon shapes in the night sky. These shapes are repeated each month.

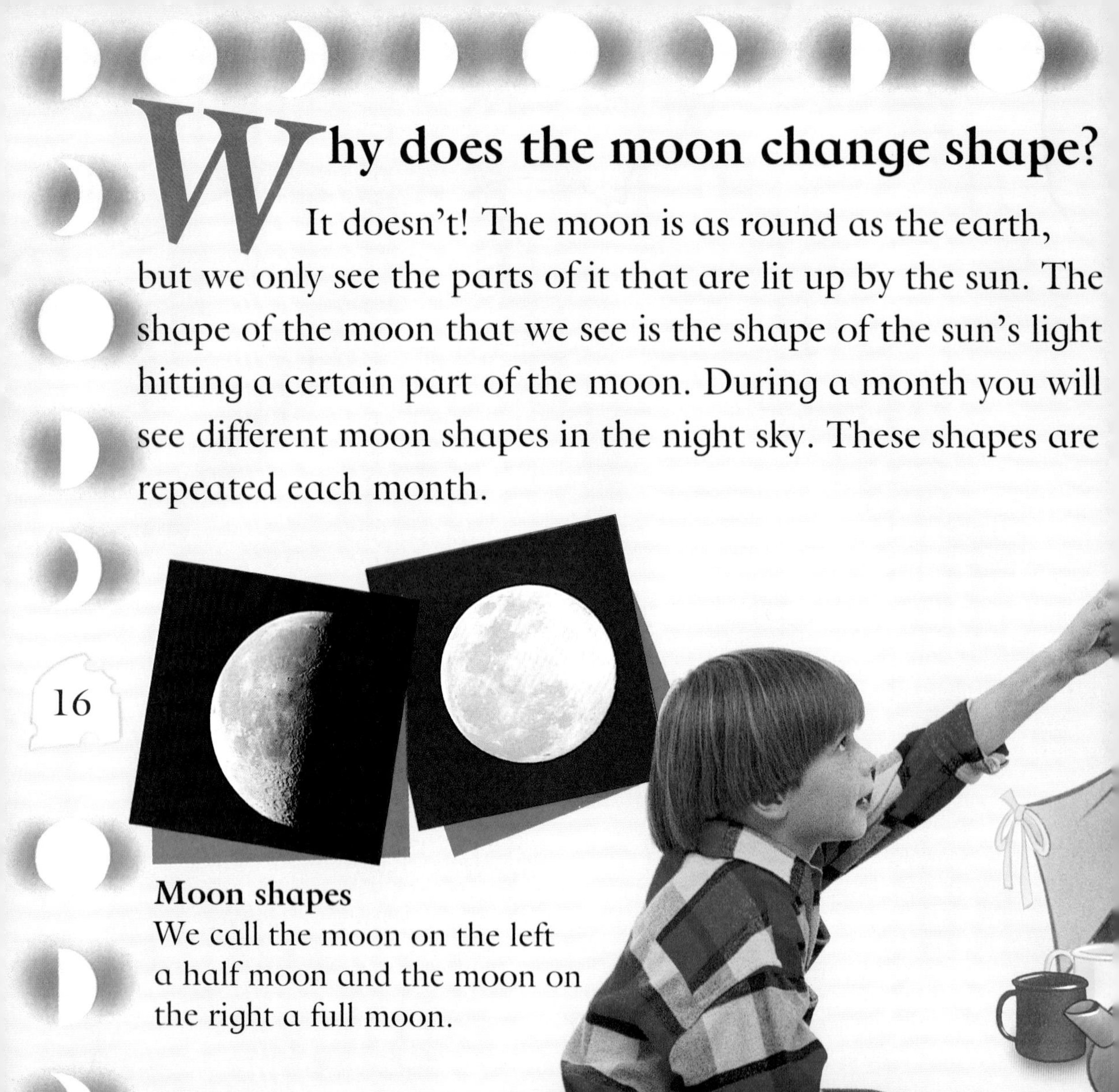

Moon shapes
We call the moon on the left a half moon and the moon on the right a full moon.

More moon facts

- Moonlight is sunlight reflected from the moon's surface.
- Until 1959, the far side of the moon had never been seen. Then in October of that year, a Russian space probe sent back the first photographs of this part of the moon.

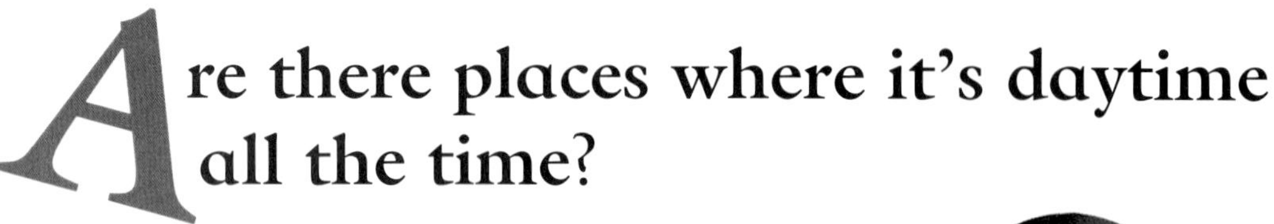

Are there places where it's daytime all the time?

Yes, during the summer months at the north and south poles. Because of the way the earth tilts, there are days in midsummer when the sun never sets, and nights in midwinter when morning never comes. Imagine that!

The land of the midnight sun
In Northern Norway, for about three months of each year, the sun shines brightly in the sky all day, and all night. Imagine going to bed when it's sunny and waking up when it's sunny!

Chilling polar facts

- There is no land under the Arctic ice at the North Pole. It is just an ice cap floating in the ocean.
- There is lots of land around the south pole called Antarctica. In fact, it's a huge ice-covered continent larger than America.

What is the equator?

It is an imaginary line around the middle of the earth, like a waistband. It divides the earth into the northern half and the southern half. The weather is always hot at the equator because it is the part of the earth closest to the sun.

Direct heat
When the sun's rays shine on the equator, they make this small area very hot. But further north and further south, the sun's rays must spread out over a bigger space. So these areas receive less heat from the sun.

Around and around
The climate at the equator is hot and rainy. That's why wonderful tropical forests grow there.

Exciting equatorial facts

At the equator, days and nights are always exactly the same length: 12 hours each.

When sailors sail across the equator they have a special celebration.

Yikes!
What time is it when an elephant sits on a fence?
Time to get a new fence.

How do flowers know it's spring?

Because in spring days start to get longer and the ground warms up. Plants and seeds that have been hiding away in the earth from the chilly winter air, react to the warmth and the light. They send up their tender shoots.

Good morning, world!
Some flowers shut their petals when it gets dark and open them up in the morning.

When the leaves fall

In the fall, as days get shorter and colder, many trees lose their leaves. They are saving their energy until spring returns.

Astonishing plant facts

Many plants take several weeks to open all their flowers.

Crocuses are so sensitive to sunlight that they close their petals if the sun goes behind a cloud.

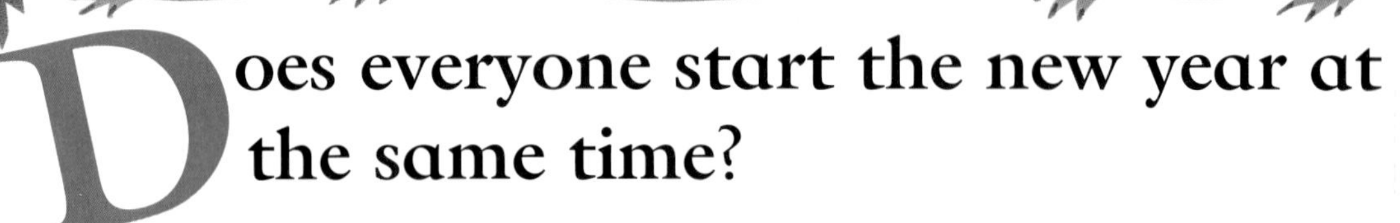

Does everyone start the new year at the same time?

No. Many of us begin our new year in January but other cultures have their new year at different times. The Chinese New Year usually begins in February. The Hebrew New Year is usually in September, and the Islamic New Year changes all the time.

Come blow your horn
The Jewish New Year is called Rosh Hashanah. People often go to the synagogue during this time. They go to think of the past year and to welcome tl new year. In the synagogue the Rabbi blows on a ram's horn, called a shofar, to welcome in the new year.

What year is it?

The Chinese calendar was invented almost 5,000 years ago by an emperor. It goes in cycles of 60 years, and each year is named after an animal. The year 2,000 will be the year of the dragon.

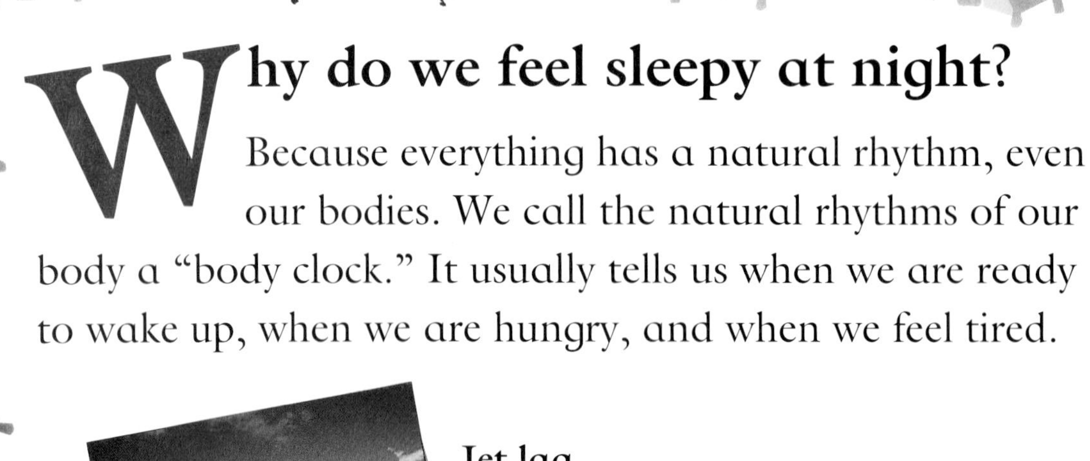

Why do we feel sleepy at night?

Because everything has a natural rhythm, even our bodies. We call the natural rhythms of our body a "body clock." It usually tells us when we are ready to wake up, when we are hungry, and when we feel tired.

Jet lag

If you travel to another time zone, your body still operates on its home time zone, and it can take quite a while to adjust.

The long sleep

Animals have body clocks too! Some have body clocks that send them to sleep all winter long. This is called hibernating.

Doctor time

Doctor, doctor, I can't get to sleep at night.

Lie on the edge of the bed and you'll soon drop off.

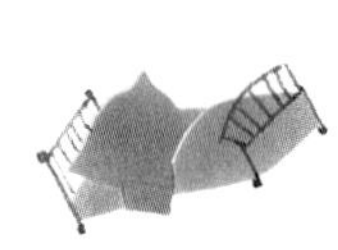

Startling snooze facts

- Not everyone's body clock is the same. People like to wake up and go to sleep at different times.
- Only people sleep on their backs, animals never do.

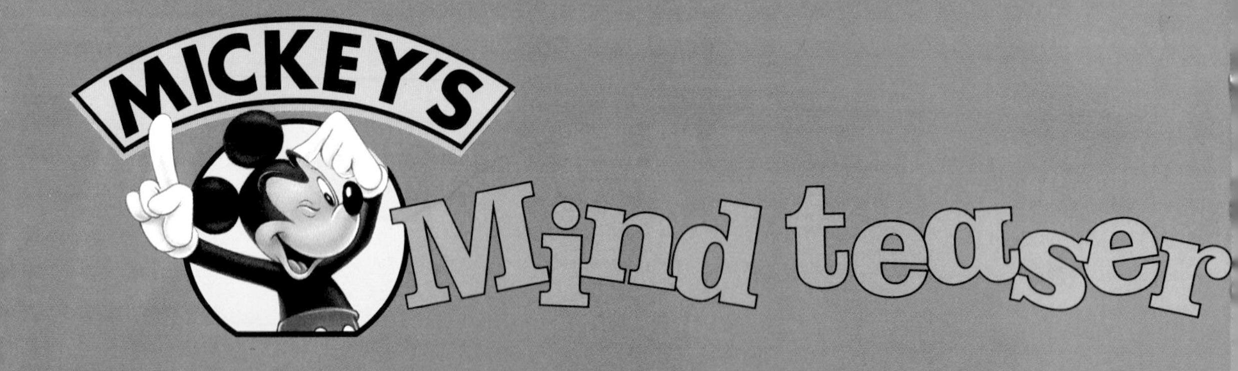

When you travel across America, you will either go backward, or forward, in time. Look at the map below to find out what time it would be in (a) San Francisco; (b) Denver; and (c) Dallas – when it's 6 o'clock in New York.

Answers: (a) 3 o'clock; (b) 4 o'clock; (c) 5 o'clock